A WREN'S ⸚

The secret link to Ble

Memoirs of a radio mechanic at Scarborough Listening Station in the Second World War

By Muriel Davison

Fellow WRENS Elizabeth Hughes (centre) with Cathie, Doreen Beresford, Rene and Joyce at Warrington in the summer of 1943

ISBN 978-0-9569987-0-5
First edition November 2011
Reprinted October 2017
Copyright © Mark Davison
No part of this publication may be reproduced or stored in a retrieval system, or transmitted in any form by any means electronically, mechanically, photocopying, recording or otherwise, without the prior written permission of the copyright owner.
Published by Mark Davison, North Bank, Smoke Lane, Reigate, Surrey RH2 7HJ. Tel: 01737 221215.
E-mail: mark.davison1@virgin.net
Edited by Nigel Davison and Mark Davison
Printed by The New Ink Printing Company, Unit 5, Seven House, 34-38 Town End, Caterham, Surrey CR3 5UG. Tel: 0208 668 7573
J. Rowntree coffee shop pictures courtesy of Scarborough Museum

A brief description of my time in the WRENS, entitled A Wren's Tale, was recorded a few years ago in a BBC Southern Counties Radio interview with presenter Bill Buckley, and can be read online on the BBC WW2 People's War archive at the following site:
http://www.bbc.co.uk/ww2peopleswar/stories/76/a4376676.shtml

A WREN'S TALE

AT the age of 17, I was working at the Colonial Office in Downing Street from January 1940, where we spent many an hour in the basement air-raid shelters during the German Blitz. I can still remember the frequent wail of the air-raid sirens. One morning, just before I reached my office, near the corner of Downing Street, the siren sounded once more and a German bomber was almost overhead. The next moment I found myself thrown flat onto the pavement, not by the bomb, but by a very kindly road sweeper, who had left his small cart and thrown himself on top of me – for my protection, of course! I was given my first brandy on reaching my desk by a very concerned member of staff.

On a later occasion I saw groups of young ladies from the Admiralty walking down Whitehall. They were WRENS in the Women's Royal Naval Service, and perhaps I was prompted by their smart navy-blue uniform to enlist in that service later in 1942. This I did shortly afterwards, signing on at Queen Anne's Gate nearby, and passed the necessary medical.

Apparently, as I had matriculated in 1939 with mathematics and physics in my school-leaving exam, I was eligible for the category of

The Gallery in Crosby Hall, Chelsea, where we dined

Radio Mechanic, and in December 1942 I became a WREN.
Initially we booked in at the sparse Mill Hill Wrennery and learnt how to scrub and polish yards of flooring. It was here that I met another new WREN, Elizabeth Hughes, who became a lifelong friend, until she sadly passed away in August 2008.

We then served together for a few weeks at Leigh-on-Sea in Essex, where we developed our scrubbing and polishing techniques in vacant flats ready for occupation by the Navy.

After this we were both billeted at Crosby Hall in Cheyne Walk, Chelsea, with about 20 other new WRENS, while we trained as future radio mechanics. This was a medieval building which had once stood in Bishopsgate and was the Great Hall of Crosby Place. However, it was moved brick by brick to Chelsea in 1910 to save it from demolition. We would dine in the Gallery and study in the evening, before returning to our digs in a modern block of flats nearby.

Attached to HMS Paragon

I WAS attached to HMS Paragon, which was a shore base in Hartlepool. Each morning our group took a coach to South East Essex Technical College at Walthamstow to study for the City and Guilds Wireless qualification, normally a two-year course, which was condensed into an intensive seven months. It certainly was hard work and some of us spent many an evening revising the day's notes to keep abreast of it all. I think our teacher was a Mr Pasque. Following this period of study, I became a Leading WREN and was presented with a new Leading WREN badge.

In the summer of 1943 my cabin mates, including Elizabeth, attended a short training course in transmitters at HMS Ariel, Warrington, Cheshire. I stayed at Crosby Hall and went up to Cheshire later with a different group of girls. It was there that I met Dorothy Harvey, who would later serve at Scarborough with me. As it turned out, we would not need to put our knowledge of transmitters to use.

While based at Chelsea, I was allowed some leave for the short journey back to my parents' home in Villiers Avenue, Surbiton. By the end of the year, the trip home would be far longer.

My first WREN hat

Back home in Surbiton

At home in Villiers Avenue, Surbiton, while on leave in 1943, with my beloved dog Chum

Posted to the Yorkshire moors

EVENTUALLY, in December 1943, I was posted to Scarborough Wireless Station on the Yorkshire moors, while my friend Elizabeth had been posted to the Fleet Air Arm Station at St Merryn, near Padstow, in Cornwall.
I have now been told that the Scarborough Wireless Station, or listening station, was newly opened and that we radio mechanics and the wireless telegraphists were the first drafting there.

I can still remember the loud whistling sound of the wind as it blew through the tall aerials outside the listening station.

Apparently these listening stations were called 'Y' stations because they were 'wireless interception' stations, and WI sounds like Y. This is mentioned in a book called The Secret Wireless War by Geoffrey Pidgeon. One reader describes the work as "filling in the gap nicely between the stories we now know of Bletchley Park and the wireless operators on the ground. It is a fascinating account of various individuals' experiences which creates a picture of this little-known group."

Billeted at the Cecil Hotel

I WAS first billeted at the Cecil Hotel at the top of Peasholm Park above the North Bay. There is now a large plaque on the outside wall in memory of about 19 WRENS and some nurses, who had been billeted there the year before us, whose boat was torpedoed and sunk while on their way to Gibraltar that year.

Later on we were billeted at Chatsworth Hotel in The Crescent, above South Bay. I remember it was rather an old-fashioned establishment and had a garden at the front. I shared a small room with a bunk bed along with Audrey King and Joyce Wooding, but we were all in and out of each other's rooms. Each day we were taken by coach or truck to the wireless station.

To this day I still have clear pictures of many details concerning these times. There were about six WREN radio mechanics in the wireless workshop, and we worked with some ex-wireless sailors, who of course were older than us 20-year-olds and much more knowledgeable too. One of my colleagues was the aforementioned

An early picture of me, Muriel Howell (now Davison) in WRENS uniform. I was attached to HMS Paragon, which was a shore base in Hartlepool

Dorothy Harvey in January 1944

Joyce Wooding pictured in 1944

Dorothy Harvey, who was about 29 at the time, but she later left when pregnant with her first daughter, Christine. Her husband Ron was an officer in the RAF.

Our work included servicing the wireless receivers which had become inoperative and had been returned from the 'receiving room'. There were many WRENS and sailors there who, as wireless telegraphists, listened in on their wireless receivers for the Morse Code messages sent out from the German U-boats at sea, and from foreign coastal stations on their Enigma machines. These messages were rushed to Bletchley Park, Buckinghamshire, by telephone or by motorcycle, often by WREN despatch riders, for decoding. The messages were received at the small gate by a sentry box, which still remains there today.

My original radio mechanic badge

My lifelong friend Elizabeth Hughes, later Parison (third from right) with Navy personnel at the Fleet Air Arm Station, St Merryn, Cornwall

*Peasholm Park boating lake, Scarborough, in the 1930s
before the start of the Second World War*

11

Peasholm Park and Pagoda, Scarborough, in 1938

Trips to London teleprinter workshops

I UNDERSTAND that Bletchley Park was chosen for the Government Decoding Centre in 1938-39 because it was at a central point in England and also had telephone cables passing down from all the main railway routes in the country. It had been derelict for a while beforehand.

While at Scarborough we radio mechanics were sent in threes to the Western Union teleprinter workshops in London for one week to learn how to service their machines. I can only remember now that they had many 'cams'. On our return, guess what? I was the one immediately sent to activate a broken-down teleprinter. It was such a relief not to be called back again, so either I must have done a good job or it was thought I was not up to the task! I assume that this was another method of sending messages to Bletchley Park.

I have one ex-WREN friend, Evelyn Irwin, who worked as a wireless telegraphist at Scarborough. I did not know her at the time, as she and my friend Rita worked in a separate room of about 100 staff. She has confirmed that taking down the German Morse Code messages was quite stressful at times, as correctness was vital for accurate decoding. She has also added the following snippets of information, which describes her work in more detail and which underlines the importance of the job at hand: *Unlike some Italian and Japanese messages, apparently all the German messages were always as clear as a bell. This was given the code QSA-5, meaning clear and perfect. There were often about five German U-boats in each group at sea, or motor torpedo boats known as schnellboots, which the Allies called E-boats, the E standing for Enemy. The German leader would give the order as to where and when they should attack the British fleet. These messages were actually picked up by our telegraphists, and it is now on record that many lives were thus saved and the war was shortened by approximately two years. Previously, so many of our ships had been sunk and sailors drowned, with much loss of food supplies from the USA. We were in such a very serious position at that time.*

My wireless telegraphist friend

ANOTHER ex-Petty Officer WREN friend of mine, Rita Hankin (née Martin), whom I met through my local WRENS Association in later life, also served at Scarborough as a wireless telegraphist. It is reported that she listened in to a German message of surrender to the British on her wireless receiver. She later married Peter Hankin, a Naval Petty Officer from the wireless station. On June 5th 1999 Rita and I attended the official dedication of the opening of the National Memorial Arboretum at Alrewas in Staffordshire. In the small WREN garden, Rita agreed to plant the first tree.

I return to the work of the radio mechanics in the wireless workshop. We tested the returned receivers for faults with ammeters and voltmeters, soldered loose joints with soldering irons (resin cored solder) and replaced faulty components like condensers (now called capacitors). We made our own screwdrivers with double steel-sprung tips for removing loose screws.

North Bay Café, Scarborough

Ron and Dorothy Harvey on their wedding day

The spa and South Bay, Scarborough

Entries from my log book

I HAVE included some images of entries from my log book. These notes, although appearing very technical in nature, will at least give an idea of the nature of the duties we undertook and maybe will be of interest to those readers who were involved in radio work.

When all seemed OK with our tests, we removed ourselves to large, earthed monkey-like cages, which excluded surrounding noise and wireless interference, and proceeded to tune our sets to the required frequency, which was rarely a quick job due to oscillations and so on. This frequency was presumably the one used by the Germans to transmit their Morse Code messages, to be picked up by our wireless telegraphists.

				BER	M
H·R·O· VALVE FEEDS. (AVERAGE)					
	VALVE	TYPE	FEED	PIN	
1ST RF	1	6D6	11·0	5	
2ND RF	2	6D6	10·0	5	
1ST DET.	3	6C6	·75	5	
L. OSC.	4	6C6	8·0	5	
1ST IF	5	6D6	6·0	5	
2ND IF	6	6D6	2·1	5	
2ND DET. AVC etc.	7	6B7	1·5	6	
2ND BFO AUDIO	8	6C6	·55	5	
BFO AUDIO	9	42	30·0	5	
RECT.	10	80	76·0	2~3 (2 diodes)	

Average valve feeds of the HRO receiver

Petty Officer M. A. Howell.
WRENS (W.R.N.S)

Radio Mechanic.

S 325a. (Established—June, 1915.)
(Revised—March, 1936.)

Delete word
not
required.

ODD }
EVEN } DAY

W/T OPERATOR'S LOG

OF

_____ OFFICE.

H.M.S. " PARAGON." R.N. SHORE WIRELESS STN
SCARBOROUGH

Delete words
not
applicable.

BAY No. _____

CABINET _____

From _____ 19

To _____ 19

_____

Sta. 1/31. Sta. 1/36.

The front cover of my operator's log book

17

LIST OF WIRELESS RECEIVERS USED

HRO – our most frequently used receiver, an American 9-tube shortwave general coverage communications receiver used by the Navy and Army.

B28 (Marconi) & B29

AR88 (RCA)

ERSKINE DST100 (Murphy) – used in tanks. Very rare.

HALLICRAFTER (SX28) – American shortwave communications receiver. Rack mounted in British Government listening posts. Used for monitoring German radar communications. I have since seen these in Mr White's Diplomatic Wireless Room.

HMS Paragon was a shore wireless station

Electric shock from a screwdriver

I DO not recall replacing many valves, but am now told by 'somebody who knows' that very few valves ever became faulty in those days. I wonder if this would be the case if valves were still in use today! I have recently seen an American RCA 807 valve of a beam tetrode design, which apparently was used in the COLOSSUS machine.

Foolishly I once plunged my screwdriver into a live set on a bench

TIME	DETAILS OF CALLS, MESSAGES, &c.	CABINET NUMBER	TIME OF ORIGIN OF MESSAGE
	8.28. TOLERANCE FIGS.		

RANGE.	FREQ.	NOISE.	DETUNE.	SENSITIVITY.	IMAGE
1.	85 kc/s.	23.5	9.	3	>100
	155 ,,	26.	9.	3	>100
2.	155 ..	15.	7.	3	>100
	420 ,,	26.5	65	3	>100
3.	500 ..	15.	55	3	>100
	1.4 Mc/s	24.5	7.	3	>100
4.	1.4 Mc/s	19.5	5.	4	100
	4.0 ..	26.5	3.	3	70
5.	4.0 ..	16.5	3.	5	84
	11.0 ..	23.0	2.	3	50
6.	11.0 ..	13.0	.75	6	50
	25.0 -	20.5	.75	4	25

Tolerance feeds of the B28 receiver

in the laboratory and received an almighty electric shock. None of the ex-sailors batted an eyelid, of course. I wondered whether they too had maybe made the same mistake at some point during their careers, but weren't going to let on!

The head of the Scarborough Y Station was a Mr Tweed, a civilian who always wore a 'plus-fours' trouser suit in a rust-coloured shade. He seemed a little shy of us WRENS. Presumably he had previously worked with 'blokes'.

TIME	DETAILS OF CALLS, MESSAGES, &c.	CABIN-ET NUM-BER	TIME OF ORIGIN OF MESSAGE

SENSITIVITY TEST.

1. Tune in signal at higher or lower end of band on RX.
   Input is from standard signal generator thro' 250Ω resistance to AE terminal I. I.S. terminals at rear are matched to 1000Ω so output from RX must be plugged into 1000Ω socket in output meter.

2. Switch off generator. Measure max. noise in D.B's on meter.

3. Detune 1st stage - shorting condenser to earth. Note reduction in meter.
   Shorting AE trimmer eliminates 1st RF stage. Most noise is generated in this stage, so low detune figs. indicate a faulty stage.

4. Turn down R.F. and A.F. gain controls to optimum position. Note meter reading. Put in 20 DB's. Switch in signal. Tune in RX. Increase input until meter gives previous reading. This gives sensitivity of RX at 20 DB signal + noise ratio.
   Reducing RF and AF gain controls to prevent overloading. Average figs. 15 DB's RF + 5 DB's AF.

5. For image protection fig. tune generator to signal twice I/F. (B28 - 4.65 K/cs). Increase generator input until original meter fig. is reached. Image protection is then read from generator attenuator in DB'S.

My sensitivity test notes for the B28 receiver

TIME	DETAILS OF CALLS, MESSAGES, &C.	CABINET NUMBER	TIME OF ORIGIN OF MESSAGE

instrument as high resistance voltmeter,
calculating feed from value of resistance.
In each case resistor is an anode
resistor, except output valve, where
resistor is in cathode lead.

AVERAGE FEEDS.

VALVE	POSITION	RESISTOR.	FEED.	
1	1st R.F.	R13	6·0 MA's.	
2	2nd R.F.	R14	6·0 "	
3	MIXER	R15	1·5 "	
4	OSC.	R7	10·0 "	200v
5	1st IF	R16	6·0 "	
6	2nd IF	R17	6·0 "	
7	3rd IF	R44	6·0 "	
8	2nd DET	R24	1·5 "	
9	OUTPUT	R30	30·0 "	15 V
10	B.F.O.	R46	1·5 "	

TOTAL H.T. 285 v. (260-300v)
Taken between pin 2 of rectifier and earth

Average feeds for the B28 receiver

B28. I.F. ALIGNMENT.

CONTROLS.
Band-pass. 1200 c/s.
Range 6.
R.F. Gain. max.
A.F. Gain. Max.
Mod. Manual.
I.F. - 465 Kc/s.

Input from ganging oscillator to grid of mixer thro' a .01 µfd condenser.
Output from Pin 5 (A.V.C. diode anode) of V8 to L.F. amp. (separate) to CRO (Y1+E,

GANGING OSCILLATOR CONTROLS.
Band-width . 50 Kc/s.
Range 4 . 465 Kc/s.
X plate terminal to X plate CRO.
Earth to earth.
Attenuator at 3.   Slide wire at 2.
Amplitude on CRO   8cm.

Phase crystal to remove subsidiary peak by loosening locking nut under I.F. Xformer 2.
Obtain max. amplitude on CRO by trimming I.F. xformers 1, 2, 3, 4 + 5. trimmers at top of 1+2, top and bottom of 3, 4 + 5.

B28 IF alignment notes

I wondered if 'blip' was a U-boat

I AM REMINDED of having my first viewing of a TV-like screen with a large 'blip' on it, and wondering if it could be a U-boat, as the men were so excited. I would have loved to ask 'sir' (Mr Tweed) whether this was so, but in those days young girls most certainly did not ask questions of their seniors. I have since read of this deferential attitude in one of the Bletchley Park books. Young people these days would be a trifle bolder!

A lighter side of our late shifts in the wireless workshop was making cheese on toast for supper – our favourite. We would melt the cheese over a Bunsen burner in an empty film tin – delicious!

By this time it had been agreed that we should work a double shift from 2pm till 11pm, in order to have a full day off duty to follow. This enabled us to visit a number of outlying towns and beauty spots, such as Whitby, Robin Hood's Bay, Filey, Bridlington, Pickering and Flamborough Head. We would visit the North Yorkshire moors and have many beautiful walks, picking primroses in the spring and sometimes visited the Falcon Inn at Cloughton, north of

Bletchley Park mansion in Buckinghamshire

Date............	DETAILS OF CALLS, MESSAGES, &c.	CABIN-ET NUM-BER	TIME OF ORIGIN OF MESSAGE
TIME			

Frequency Range.

50 K/cs - 30 M/cs.   7 ranges.

IF's

2 IF's - 2 Mc/s and 110 K/cs.

2 Mc/s.

Ranges A-F. RX operates as double superhet on first five positions of selectivity. As single superhet. in 'broad' position of selectivity.

110 K/s

Range G. RX operates as single superhet. 'Broad' position is inoperative.

Variable selectivity provided at following bandwidths.

Sharp.   1 K/cs.

2   .   1·4 ..

3   .   1·6 ..

4   .   1·8 ..

5   .   2·0 ..

broad   12 - 25 K/cs.

Input.

matched to 75 n or 600 n as reqd.

Output.

4000 n for H.R. phones.

600 n line.

BFO

When switched on, automatically switches off AVC and does not operate in 'broad' pos. of selectivity.

Erskine DST 100 particulars

24

Me in casual wear while off duty

Long after the war, The Falcon Inn, Cloughton, continued to offer visitors refreshments in the 1960s

Scarborough, for a lunch of bacon, two eggs and chips – the best ever! The inn still remains there today.

Chickens smuggled out

IN SCARBOROUGH town centre we enjoyed many a similar meal in the restaurants. There must have been plenty of chickens around. Our poor mothers at home were only allowed one egg per week, or occasionally two. One Christmas, having home leave (we were allowed three 10-day breaks per year), I managed to smuggle two chickens (plucked and innards removed) from the local butcher, and shoved them into a suitcase on the train rack, to take home to Mum for Christmas dinner – please don't report me!

TYPICAL FIGS. FOR D.S.T. 100 TAKEN AT SCARBOROUGH. MAY 1944.

BAND	FREQ	SENS'Y S/N		20DB NOISE		FEEDS		GAIN IN	RED'S DBS
		BEFORE	AFTER	BEFORE	AFTER	VALVE	MAs.	RF.	AF.
A	25	2·4	1·25	-2	3	VIA	13·5	0 0	0 10
	19	1·8	1·45	-2	3	2A	4·2	0 0	0 10
	13	2·0	2·5	-1	3	3A	7·5	0 0	0 10
B	11	1·0	1·05	8	17	3B	9·4	0 0	10 10
	8	1·0	1·0	8	16	4A	2·25	0 0	11 10
	5	1·2	1·15	-1	12	2B	7·7	0 0	11 10
C	4·5	1·0	{1·0	23	31	5A	6·4	5 0	15 2
	3·25	1·3	1·3	16	25	4B	3·35	05	10 15
	2·0	1·3	1·7	20	>32	3C	·14	05	10 15
D	1800	1·15	1·7	18	25	6A	2·25	0 0	10 20
	1320	1·15	1·35	22	29	7A	-	0 0	15 20
	830	1·35	1·35	15	32	8A	0·3	0 0	10 25
E	720	1·4	1·4	31	31	9A	4·2	5 0	20 25
	530	1·45	1·45	31	31			5 0	20 25
	330	1·9	1·65	28	32			5 0	15 25
F	290	2·0	1·6	>34	>32	TOTAL I	9·4	5 0	20 25
	210	1·7	1·75	>34	>32	HT·VOLTS	230	5 0	20 20
	130	2·1	2·1	32	>32			5 0	20 25
G	116	2·0	1·8	18	25			0 0	10 20
	84	2·1	1·8	19	25			0 0	10 20

Sensitivity in microvolts input from sig/gen. Noise in db above 1 MW.

Figures for the Erskine DST 100 which I recorded at Scarborough in May 1944

Off duty in Scarborough with Dorothy Harvey

Dancing at the Royal Hotel

W E ENJOYED many an evening dancing at the Royal Hotel in Scarborough and at the Olympic Dance Hall on the South Promenade. Latterly we were allowed to wear civilian clothes when off duty, and especially for dances. I wore a red dress I made at classes held in our quarters, which was a welcome change from navy blue. I used my clothes coupons for the material, which were intended for use in replacing our long navy-blue woollen knickers! The dress shop was Johnson's.

In the summer of 1944 my family were staying at Scarborough, having a welcome rest from the London bombing. I was shocked to see my father looking so worn out and grey-faced. In addition to his daily job at the Swiss Bank in Byfleet, Surrey, where the bank had transferred from the City due to the London air raids, he undertook local ARP (Air Raid Precaution) warden duties two nights a week, and this must have taken its toll on him. The seaside holiday, however, did him a world of good.

The Open-Air Theatre and pleasure park, Scarborough

My family and friends stayed here at Dunvegan Manor,
a private guest house, in Scarborough, in 1944

At the Scarborough Open-Air Theatre, in the small Northstead Manor Gardens, we saw A Midsummer Night's Dream. Some of the actors were performing from a small boat as it sailed up along the narrow stream. My sister Doreen has now reminded me how impressed they all were at the very strong Yorkshire accent of the actors. Having lived among Yorkshire folk for quite a while, I had never even noticed!

Christmas away from home

WE ALSO spent many hours on the lovely beaches when off duty and enjoyed swimming in the North and South Bays. While at the Cecil Hotel, we gave a "party for the Poles". The Polish airmen and army were stationed nearby. Some good snacks were rustled up and there was dancing too. Much has been recorded about the bravery of our Polish allies and I think we all recognised their contribution at the time. It wasn't easy having a conversation with these lads, but I think they knew a

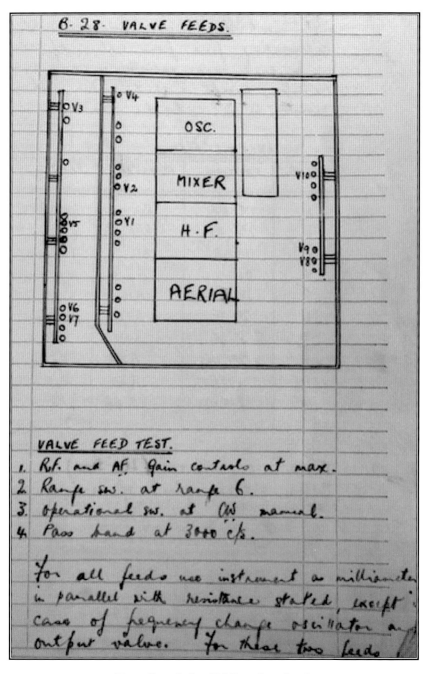

B-28. VALVE FEEDS.

OSC.

MIXER

H·F.

AERIAL

VALVE FEED TEST.

1. R.F. and A.F. Gain controls at max.
2. Range sw. at range 6.
3. Operational sw. at CW manual.
4. Pass band at 3000 c/s.

For all feeds use instrument as milliameter in parallel with resistance stated, except in case of frequency change oscillator and output valve. For these two feeds

Details of the B28 valve feeds

little English by then.

We spent our first Christmas at Scarborough and enjoyed a great dinner, served by the WREN officers. The afternoon and evening was spent in a local pub and some of the ladies were dancing on the tables. It was all fun, but of course nothing like our family Christmases. I did miss my mum and dad!

In 1944, I seemed to be the only WREN who caught German measles. How very unpatriotic! I was taken by truck over the moors and arrived at a small hospital near Whitby, which turned out to be an empty primary school. My companions were a sailor, a soldier and a WREN officer. We all had to sit on the infant chairs at an infants' table for our meals. This was very uncomfortable for the men, but it caused a few laughs, which cheered me up.

I also recall giving a blood donation, lying on the floor in a glass conservatory (now demolished). My blood donor's card is still with me, but with very ragged edges (rather like me at 89 years of age at the time of writing).

Workshops with Bunsen burners

ALL we radio mechanics were promoted to WREN Petty Officer for the last year or two of our service, and so were able to wear those tri-cornered hats, with our white shirts and brass buttons. For work we wore the real sailors' bell bottoms with buttoned flap fronts, navy-blue shirts and round caps.

I often think back to that large wooden workshop where we

On home leave in Villiers Avenue, Surbiton, in the spring of 1945.
By this time, I had been promoted to Petty Officer.
Note the tri-cornered hat which I was now permitted to wear

*My leading
WREN badge*

*One of the Petty
Officer brass buttons
I have kept*

*My Petty Officer
badge I still own*

*Sporting bell-bottoms, at home in
Surbiton, spring 1945*

worked, a short walk away from the underground listening station itself.

I can still envisage the large wooden worktops, the stools and the Bunsen burners.

The place resembled a chemistry laboratory, and all of us had our own set of tools and equipment. At one end were large windows,

A march-past of WRENS in Scarborough in early 1943. Audrey King is on the far left of the second row. Dorothy Harvey is on the far right of the front row

with smaller ones along each side of the hut.

Up to half a dozen radio mechanics and a similar number of retired Navy wireless operators worked in there at any one time. The gentlemen had the luxury of an inside lavatory, but we girls had to use an outside toilct.

Wonderful news from Mr Churchill

O N THE afternoon of May 8th 1945, we were all gathered together to hear the wonderful news on the wireless from Mr Churchill that the war was finally over, and so our country (and many others) was at peace at last. This was VE Day (Victory in Europe Day). I called my parents in Surbiton and they were overjoyed at the good news. It had been a particularly hard few years in London and the suburbs, especially for my father who had fought in the First World War.

During that evening we radio mechanics, still in uniform, of course,

Happy faces all round. VE Day, May 8th 1945. Back row (left to right): Joyce Parish, Freda Whitwell, Robin Smith and me. Front row (left to right): Joyce Wooding and Audrey King. Robin later lived in Windsor, Berkshire, and although I did make contact with her in later years, a meeting never materialised

Outside Chatsworth Hotel, The Crescent, Scarborough, on VE Day, May 8th 1945. Back row (left to right): Audrey King and Joyce Wooding. Front row (left to right): Me, Joyce Parish, Freda Whitwell and Robin Smith

Joyce Parish in the early summer of 1945.
She had the most lovely brown eyes

At the wireless station at Irton Moor, Scarborough, with Ted, our driver. From left to right: Joyce Parish, Joyce Wooding, Audrey King, Freda Whitwell, name unknown, and me. The picture was taken in 1944

went into Scarborough where there was dancing in the streets and great jubilation, as there was everywhere. Flags and bunting bedecked the streets in the town centre.

Navy Rum is still a favourite tipple

THE roads and pavements were full of locals as well as WRENS and sailors, and the pubs were all crammed with happy people. We later visited a pub where I enjoyed a Navy Rum or two. In those days, we did not dare drink a lot! Today Navy Rum is still one of my favourite tipples.

In the early summer of 1945, I took some leave and travelled by train to Weston-super-Mare in Somerset, where I joined up with my

Freda Whitwell in May 1945

Mum and Dad at home in Surbiton in the spring of 1945

41

*With my mother, Elsie, and father, Ernie, and younger sister,
Doreen (far right) while on holiday in Somerset
in the summer of 1945*

parents and sister Doreen for a welcome break.

Victory in Japan followed in the summer of 1945 and we all took
part in a church parade to celebrate VJ Day on Sunday August 15th
1945.

In late 1945, we WRENS used to queue each evening at an off-
licence for a tot of Navy Rum and the shop assistant would put it in
a small bottle, which we transferred into a larger bottle. I then took
the bottle home at Christmas as a treat, which horrified my parents!
Demobilisation did not come until December 31st 1945, as I guess
there were many clearing-up jobs to be dealt with first.

Despite the war and some inevitable sad stories, I have great memories of that time. I feel glad to have at last made my first full record
of all these events, which hopefully will give my family and anyone
who wishes to read it a clearer picture of life in Scarborough at that
time.

*Enjoying time with my mother and sister Doreen
at Weston-super-Mare in 1945*

*Mum and Dad, feeling happy and relaxed at
Weston-super-Mare, in the summer of 1945*

Losing touch with friends

AFTER we all returned home on December 31st 1945, I lost touch with my former friends. Most of them had married earlier and settled into a new life. Joyce Parish apparently emigrated to New Zealand. I met my future husband Norman Davison while on demobilisation leave, when he returned to England after several years in Burma serving in the Royal Air Force. It was therefore a happy ending for me as well, and we were married for 62 years.

In my 1940s overcoat   *My future husband, Norman Davison*

Settling down near Surbiton

WE SETTLED down in Hook, near Surbiton, Surrey, where I still live today, and had three children, Mark, Susan and Nigel, who are a great support to me, and four lovely grandchildren. My husband sadly died on Good Friday, 2010, but I just try to remember all the happy times we shared.

I have visited Scarborough on several occasions with my family since the war and still enjoyed it immensely, while my connection with the WRENS still continues today. We 'old' WRENS have had monthly meetings for 18 years at the Kingston-upon-Thames branch of the Association of WRENS. Sadly our numbers are diminishing now, as many of us wartime girls are of a good age, in our late 80s and 90s.

Evelyn Irwin and Rita Hankin (both of whom I mentioned earlier) have both been members of this branch for many years. Margaret Moreton, a special friend of mine, whom I have known for many years, has also been a regular member. She served as a post-war WREN Petty Officer Writer for ten years before marrying John Moreton, an ex-Naval Officer who served in the last war.

J. Rowntree & Sons, tea and coffee dealers, in Westborough, Scarborough, and its coffee lounge which we frequented

VJ Day church parade in Scarborough,
Sunday August 15th 1945.
I am in the centre of the third row from the rear

A reunion in Scarborough

MURIEL Kent (née Jeal and formerly Lorenzini) joined the WRENS at the outbreak of war in 1939 and was posted to Sandy Lane in Scarborough, where she lived initially in private lodgings, before the opening of the wireless station. She was later commissioned as a Code and Cypher Officer and was posted to Canada and the USA. On October 2nd 2000, Rita, Muriel and I attended an enjoyable reunion with ex-Scarborough 'old' sailors at the Cumberland Hotel in Scarborough.

I have regularly represented the WRENS at Remembrance Day services over the years, both in Whitehall and, more locally, in Kingston-upon-Thames, although I have now had to give my legs a rest! On November 11th 2001, with my branch colleagues Stella and Joyce, I laid a wreath on the war memorial in Union Street, Kingston-upon-Thames, which was pictured in the Richmond and Twickenham Times.

In March 2005 I was awarded the Freedom of Bletchley Park which gives me free access 'in recognition of my contribution to the work

Audrey and husband Nev, a Scarborough man who served in the Army, on their wedding day towards the end of the war

Freda with her husband Norman on the day they married close to the end of the war

With Rita (centre) and Muriel Kent (right) at the Cumberland Hotel, Scarborough, in 2000

undertaken at Bletchley Park during the Second World War', which I consider a truly great honour and privilege. I have visited the mansion on several occasions and found it most interesting. It amazes me to think that I may have assisted in some small way the work which was undertaken there in the fight to break the Nazi code. Little did we realise the significance of our work at the time.

Dinners at quarters cooked by stewards

O F COURSE I often reminisce fondly about my wartime days in Yorkshire. Sometimes, little extra memories are stirred by events. Only recently I recalled regularly going to the café in the rather classy J. Rowntree & Sons, tea and coffee merchants, at 20-21 Westborough, Scarborough, where I would enjoy a coffee.

I also remember having all the dinners cooked for us by stewards

Norman and I after our diamond wedding celebration near Dorking in 2007

at the quarters – roast dinners and the like. I was sure food supplies were far more plentiful than at home!

I did go into the listening station once to carry out an errand and remember staff listening to German messages.

Another anecdote I can add is that the retired ex-Navy staff working in my hut wore beige overalls. They were in their 40s,, which at the time seemed old to me.

In writing this account, I hope I have provided an insight, however small, into the secretive but vital operations at the listening station at Scarborough. I myself have just turned 89 years of age at the time of recording this, my very own WREN'S tale.

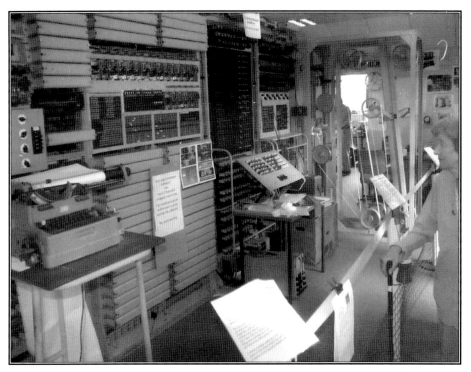

Marvelling at the COLOSSUS machine on a recent visit to Bletchley Park

Preparing to place the wreath of commemoration at Kingston's memorial on November 11th 2001, with Stella and Joyce, as reported in the Richmond and Twickenham Times of November 16th 2001

Enjoying tea in May 2011 at Pembroke Lodge,
Richmond Park, Surrey

53

Relaxing with members of the Kingston upon Thames WRENS Association at a garden party in the summer of 2005 at the home of member Pam Lawler. I am second from right in the bottom row between my friends, Elizabeth Parison (left) and Margaret Moreton (right)

My original WRENS hat which I still own today

My dear friend, Margaret Moreton, in 2007

STATION X BLETCHLEY PARK

Freedom of Bletchley Park

This is to certify that Bletchley Park Trust hereby grants

free access to Bletchley Park whilst it is open to the public

to

MURIEL ALICE DAVISON

in recognition of his/her contribution to the work

undertaken at Bletchley Park during World War II.

Signed on behalf of Bletchley Park Trust.

C.J. Charm

Date: 22nd March 2005

Bletchley Park Trust

My Freedom of Bletchley Park certificiate awarded in 2005

On a visit to Bletchley Park several years ago, the museum curator urged me to write down all my wartime experiences in the WRENS. As a result I have recorded all my memoirs in this little publication. I would like to thank my family, my friends in the WRENS Association, and Gillian Mason at Bletchley Park for all their encouragement and support.

Muriel Alice Davison (née Howell),
Hook, Chessington, Surrey
October 2011